A SHORT
HISTORY OF SEX

A
SHORT
HISTORY
OF
SEX

BY RICHARD ARMOUR

Lovingly Illustrated by Campbell Grant

McGraw-Hill Book Company
New York   Toronto   St. Louis   San Francisco
Dusseldorf   Mexico   Panama

Library of Congress
Catalog Card Number: 71-124133

SECOND PRINTING, NOVEMBER, 1970

02263

ACKNOWLEDGMENTS

The genesis, as well as the exodus, of this book was an article in *National Lampoon,* "Sex through the Ages," subsequently revised and expanded. Use has also been made of portions of my article, "Sex in the Stone Age," that originally appeared in *Playboy* and is copyright © 1966 by HMH Publishing Co., Inc. I am grateful for permission to include this material.

R.A.

A SHORT
HISTORY OF SEX

It takes two

· I ·

THE BEGINNINGS

Sex has come to loom so large in modern society that it seems timely to consider its origins and examine it in historical perspective. The survey that follows touches only the high spots.[1] It is hoped that this brief study will open the way to further exploration by psychologists, sociologists, sexologists, and publishers of pornography.

The word sex comes from the Latin *sexus,* meaning division, and is akin to the verb *secare,* to cut.[2] From this it may be gathered that it takes two to make sex. In the Biblical account of the Creation, as long as Adam was the only human

[1] Some of which respond interestingly to the touch.

[2] In French, *sexe* is a four-letter word. This is the sort of thing you might expect from the French.

being on earth there was no such thing as sex.[1]
Thus there was no incentive to discuss Adam's
virility, his libido, birth control, or the constitu-
tionality of sex education. The cutting apart of
Adam (see *secare,* above) to remove a rib and
make of it a creature named Eve was the beginning of sex as we know it today.[2]

Eve's eating of the Forbidden Fruit did not,
therefore, create sex but only the awareness of it.
"I was unaware of it before," Eve said to Adam.
Adam, who was listening none too closely and
thought she said "underwear," suddenly realized
that they were both stark naked.[3] Instead of turn-
ing tail, however, Adam turned tailor. He deftly
fashioned for himself a leafweight suit, suitable
for year-around wear in Eden. How he managed
to keep it on, this being before the invention of

[1] Except among the lower animals, where sex is known as
mating, is often seasonal rather than the year around, and by
human standards shows little imagination.

[2] Conversion of a rib into a creature with ingenious new
erogenous zones goes beyond anything yet achieved by modern science.

[3] The folk belief that babies are brought by the stork probably had its origin in the confusion of "a stork, naked" and
"stark naked."

Beginning of sex

Scotch tape, glue, and thumbtacks, still perplexes
fashion designers and structural engineers.
It may have had something to do
with Adam's underpinning,
though any pinning over
or under had to be

No zipper, no buttons

done with exquisite care and a steady hand.[1]

This event marks not only a great leap forward by sex but the origin of the clothing industry. Henceforth, at least up to the era of nudist colonies and topless, bottomless, and middleless entertainers, sex and clothing were to be closely related, working hand in hand, hand in glove, and sometimes tongue in cheek.[2]

The sex life of Adam and Eve is a matter of conjecture only. No first-hand or first-eye account has been left us by an inquisitive neighbor. No door-to-door poll was taken, and there was no equivalent of the Kinsey Report. Had there been, it would have been relatively simple to figure out average scores and to determine the frequency according to education, occupation, and rural or urban. We can be sure, however, that Adam was never stimulated by prurient literature, erotic centerfolds, or stag movies. For her part, Eve had no

[1] Could it have been capillary attraction? Anyhow, there was no zipper. There were no buttons. It was all or nothing.

[2] Imagine, if you can, a double-breasted figleaf.

cause for jealousy. If Adam tired of her, there was no "other woman." Wife swapping was unheard of.[1]

[1] Adam may have had a glimmer of the idea when he thought of trading Eve for a nice plump cow. But he knew the bull would have none of it.

No first-hand account

Tempter

Eve, of course, had been tempted and had succumbed. Her tempter was a serpent, and how she could have fallen for that hairless, chinless creature is difficult to comprehend. Perhaps it was because she was so inexperienced. Her circle of male companions included only Adam, who provided a limited basis for comparison. It must be remembered, too, that the serpent did nothing more to Eve than persuade her to do something naughty, something against her moral code.[1]

That, however, was sufficient for the serpent. As Eve bit into the forbidden fruit, he writhed ecstatically. He had his own, somewhat peculiar way of getting his kicks. Obviously he was an apple fetishist.[2]

Once Eve acquired the taste, she was unable to stop. "An apple a day," she said to herself, "is hardly enough." Soon she was eating apples, one after another, from morning till night. So preoccu-

[1] The male population being what it was, Eve can hardly be accused of promiscuity. Prostitution, moreover, had not yet arrived. Though it was to become the oldest profession, it had to wait, sex at that time being untainted by professionalism.

[2] And rotten to the core. Getting Eve hooked on apples, he has the dubious distinction of being the first pusher.

pied was she with her gnawing and chomping that Adam found her poor company. He had to think up something they could do together. . . .

This much we can say for Adam and Eve, with regard to sex: they were pioneers.

Pioneers

·II·

SEX IN THE STONE AGE

Our Stone Age ancestors may have been ignorant about some things, such as iron and bronze, not to mention titanium, but they knew about sex. They may even have known as much about it as we do, at least the fundamentals, which is something one hates to admit about such primitive people.[1] There were, after all, no sudden breakthroughs in sex comparable to the rapid advance in transportation after the invention of the wheel. In all likelihood, sex very early reached a plateau, and a graph of the history of sex, from the day of its discovery, would look something like this:

```
                                          ─TODAY
  ┌─────────────────────────────────────
  │
DAY OF DISCOVERY
```

[1] Nor did they learn about it in novels and sex manuals. (At one time these, which today are interchangeable, were different kinds of books.)

The popular concept of sex in the Stone Age [1] is of a man beating a woman over the head with a club, seizing her by the hair, and dragging her off to a cave. In cartoons, which are the chief source of this concept, the woman is soft, bosomy, and appealing, about a 38-23-36, while the man is hairy, snaggle-toothed, and badly dressed.[2]

[1] And a popular concept it is, especially among men.

[2] A woman's measurements, if made at all, were probably made with a vine, knotted at regular intervals. A woman with a 38-knot bosom would seem to be going somewhere, and fast.

Popular concept

21

How the first cartoonist got such an idea, which has been passed along by hundreds of cartoonists since, one can only surmise. Perhaps the cartoonist himself was hairy, snaggle-toothed, and badly dressed, a man who had had no luck whatsoever with women, and his cartoon was a bit of sex fantasy and wish fulfillment. Whatever his motivation, by establishing a precedent for the cartoonists who followed him, he fixed in the minds of millions of men a picture of sex in the Stone Age

Wish fulfillment

which, as we shall prove, was erroneous and did a great disservice to our forebears.[1]

Is it credible that a man would hit a woman over the head with a club considerably larger than a baseball bat when he could have knocked her out with his fist? Of course not. And yet the cartoons repeatedly show the man not only having knocked the woman unconscious with his club but still holding the club in one hand while with the other he drags her to the place of rendezvous.

It should be apparent to anyone who has read Freud that the club was a phallic symbol. The woman was not hit over the head with it. She was simply shown it. What struck her was the enormity of the situation. She was overcome. She swooned.[2]

[1] In belated justice, we should form some such organization as Fair Play for Stone Age Man, or FPSAM, contributions to which would be tax deductible. Members would stop people on the street and ask them, sternly, "Are you guilty of spreading lies and misinformation about the sex life of Stone Age man?" This would lead to meaningful dialogue, involvement, and in many instances conversion.

[2] There can be no doubt about it. The club was for display purposes only, and further proof, if proof is needed, that men have been boastful and prone to exaggerate from earliest times.

Symbol

And what of the suggestion, endlessly repeated
in cartoons, that once the woman was in no posi-
tion to resist (that is to say, flat on her back), she
was grabbed by the hair and pulled to the nearest
cave? This is ridiculous on the face of it.[1] It was
the Stone Age, remember, and the ground was ter-
ribly stony. It was quite different from pulling a
woman along, say, a paved road or a sidewalk. A

[1] Or, in this instance, on the back of it.

woman dragged even a hundred yards over bumpy ground would hardly be at her best.[1]

Stone Age man was no modern sedentary type. He was fully capable of picking up a woman and carrying her in his arms. What if he had to set her down occasionally to rest? It would be relaxing for both of them, and a chance to get acquainted. They might, in fact, find a pile of fermented berries, while resting under a bush, and eat themselves into a devil-may-care state, completely freed of inhibitions. In fact they might never get to the cave.[2]

[1] First an unsightly bump on her head and then a raw and bleeding back. This is the sort of thing that kills desire.

[2] Indeed the nearest cave might be occupied by another pair of lovers, and it would be a mile or more to a cave with a VACANCY sign.

Pickup

Discovery of caves with erotic drawings of pre-historic animals on the walls [1] should not be taken as convincing proof that caves were places of seduction, the equivalent of the modern bachelor apartment. Such caves may simply have been the studios of avant-garde artists whose sex lives took a peculiar turn in that they were voyeurs, but of animals rather than women. Having glimpsed a nude mastodon bathing, or watched the mating of two rather passionate saber-toothed tigers, they lost no time getting back to their studios and sketching the lurid details on their walls.[2]

We hope the reader now has a better understanding of sex life in the Stone Age, and that certain unfortunate misconceptions have been set straight.

[1] Shamelessly naked, all of them.
[2] The original graffiti. Given time, today's drawings on privy walls may also be considered art.

Erotic drawings

Fertile land

· III ·

SEX IN EGYPT

Egypt lies on both sides of the Nile. But the ancient Egyptians, as archaeologists have discovered, were not wont to lie on their sides so much as on their backs. This probably should tell us something about their sex life, at least that of their mummies. It was a fertile land.

The Sphinx had a secret, known as the Secret of the Sphinx, that he kept close-mouthed about.[1] It was probably something nasty he did as an adolescent.[2]

What went on behind the pyramids we can only imagine.

[1] A good idea, anyhow, with all those sandstorms.

[2] If he had followed the example of the author of *Portnoy's Complaint,* he would not only have told about it but made a fortune describing every intimate detail.

Graffiti were cunningly written in hieroglyphics so that tourists would not know and be embarrassed. In the early nineteenth century, however, a translation was made by Rosetta Stone.[1] Today this is kept in the British Museum, along with other erotica, for the benefit of Egyptologists, curators, and other dirty old men. With the invention of papyrus, smut [2] could be distributed in books and pamphlets which could be sent through the mails more cheaply and unobtrusively than tablets of stone. Pornography, previously limited to cornerstones, would soon be available in the corner drugstore.

The Pharaohs were half god and half man, roughly corresponding to Upper and Lower Egypt. Had the Pharaohs been all god, there is no telling what would have happened to their sex life. As a matter of fact, sex was none too easy for some of the Egyptian gods and goddesses, many

[1] *Nee* Rose Stein.

[2] Had you ever realized that smut is Tums spelled backward?

of whom had animal or bird heads. A loving peck from such as Thoth, the ibis-headed deity, could cost an eye.[1]

[1] And it was hardly worth it, producing as it did very little erotic stimulation.

Loving peck

First conquest

The sex goddess [1] of ancient Egypt was Cleopatra. She mostly sat around in a see-through skirt and a brass bra, planning conquests. [2] Her first conquest was of Julius Caesar, a man about thirty years her senior. [3] He was stout and balding, wear-

[1] Though all woman. There was nothing half and half about *her*.

[2] In battle she often wore no bra at all, hoping to draw fire from the enemy. Once the fire was drawn from them, they were docile and helpless.

[3] Thus setting a precedent for the marriage of Hollywood starlets to producers, agents, plastic surgeons, and others who can further their careers.

ing a crown of laurel leaves in lieu of a hairpiece, and had little to commend him but his being an Emperor, while Cleopatra was only a Queen.[1] He carried her off to Rome, together with other spoils, and spoiled her.

Her second noteworthy conquest was of Mark Antony. When they met, in 42 B.C., after the battle of Philippi, she was dressed as Aphrodite, the Greek goddess of Love. Antony, who knew his mythology and had an eye for cleavage, took the hint. The fact that he was married did not stop him. After all, his wife was back in Rome and he was in Asia Minor on business and wondering what to do on weekends.[2]

Cleopatra came to a bad end, as do some women (but not all) who play around with married men. She secured an asp, which in those days you could get without a prescription, and coaxed it to give her a poisonous bite. At first, when she placed it on her arm, the asp refused to do her bidding. But when she placed it against her

---

[1] Cleopatra was hospitable to visiting royalty. "My queen-size bed," she would purr, "is big enough for two."

[2] Another precedent was set. See Arthur Miller's *Death of a Salesman.*

Second conquest

breast, the asp thought to himself (he was a male asp), "Oh, what the heck!" [1]

Egypt's greatest contribution to sex after Cleopatra was the belly dancer. By causing a tassel attached to her navel to rotate first clockwise and then counterclockwise, a belly dancer makes time stand still.[2]

---

[1] Some herpetologists think the asp, a small venomous snake, was the horned viper *Cerastes cornutus*. Anyhow Cleopatra's asp, called "Lucky" by his friends, is a classic example of being at the right place at the right time. No other asp has simultaneously done so much for history and for himself.

[2] But men in the audience get fidgety. A belly dancer is not to be confused with a ballet dancer. For one thing, a ballet dancer may be a male, and then again he may not.

Secured an asp

Admired an urn

·IV·

SEX AMONG THE GREEKS AND ROMANS

The Greeks were great lovers of beauty, and it is hard to believe that they admired only friezes and urns.[1] It was an age of manliness, and Greeks were always quick to show their prowess. Though this was long before Freud, there can be no doubt that the columns (pillars, shafts) on the buildings atop the Acropolis, erected by men, had a function beyond that of holding up roofs and pediments. The Greeks, fond as they were of symbolism, were trying to tell us something.[2]

[1] A common design showed a girl being pursued by a satyr, a woodland demigod having the ears, horns, legs, and no telling what else of a goat. A horny old satyr was, in fact, very much like an old goat, always pursuing young women around and around urns and things.

[2] The abduction of Helen, as told with classical restraint by Homer, is the sort of thing that even today helps the cir-

The Greek gods should have been above carnal lust, but Zeus was forever donning a disguise and going after some innocent young maiden.[1] Sex was not only extra-marital but extra-human.[2] A beautiful young Greek woman who had not been ravished by a god or two must have had little to talk about to her masseuse.

---

culation of certain magazines and of their readers. Sex was so rampant in Greek drama that many ancient plays, if shown in a movie version, would have to be labeled Restricted.

[1] The time he dressed up as a bull and carried off Europa he was really in character.

[2] They believed in a little something extra.

Carnal lust

Sabine women

And the Spartans were not practicing physical culture just to fight better. They might sleep on a bed of nails—but not *every* night.

As for the Romans, one need only examine a painting of the "Rape of the Sabine Women," looking closely at the details, to realize that when Roman men went out to get wives they were impatient with any long period of courting. They knew what they wanted [1] and wasted no time getting it. Moreover, the Sabine women didn't have to accept the invitation to the festival. They must have known what was going to happen after the Romans had had a few drinks.[2]

Roman men being as they were, it was no easy thing for the Vestal virgins to remain virgins. One thing that helped was keeping busy tending the perpetual fire on the altar of Vesta. Another was staying away from men. Still another was knowing that if they lost their chastity they would be buried alive.[3]

[1] The buxom type.

[2] I have carefully examined the expression on the faces of the Sabine women in one of the famous paintings of this event, and have come to the conclusion that it was not rape.

[3] No wonder there were only six women in all Rome in this line of work.

The public baths in Rome contributed greatly to clean bodies and dirty minds. The Roman chariot, however, was a poor place for love-making, having no back seat.[1]

Venus was the goddess of love. From Venus we get venereal disease.[2]

Borrowing from the Dionysian rites of the Greeks, the Romans developed the orgy to a high point of eating, drinking, and unadulterated [3] sex. Interestingly, the word orgy goes back, with a few detours, to the Greek *ergon,* meaning work. Had you told this to a Roman, lying on his back while a beautiful slave-maiden dropped grapes into his mouth, he would have said, in Latin,[4] "You're kidding." [5]

---

[1] It was open in the front, too, and the presence of those horses was embarrassing.

[2] That is, we get the word venereal.

[3] Though often adulterous.

[4] And Vulgar Latin, at that.

[5] However one definition of work is "Exertion of strength or faculties for the accomplishment of something." This would seem to apply very well to sex.

Virgins and perpetual fire

One final thought. Had Roman women declined more, Rome would have declined less.

Orgy

Honorable

· V ·

SEX IN THE
MIDDLE AGES

Sex in the Middle Ages was governed by the Code of Chivalry. This meant that anything a knight could do without getting off his horse (*cheval*) was all right. Even off his horse, if he kept on his suit of armor he was trustworthy (or rustworthy), honorable, and ingenious.[1]

A knight could win a woman's favors by going on a pilgrimage, winning a joust, or slaying a dragon.[2] Having done any of the three, he would present himself to his lady fair and ask, "Prithee, milady, how about those favors?" The lady would drop a glove, and maybe at the same time her

[1] A medieval maiden carrying a can opener was probably not thinking of defending herself.

[2] Or a dragoon, the name given to a heavily equipped cavalryman.

47

Chaste

eyes. If the knight failed to catch them she would
send him on another mission, or perhaps a Cru-
sade, taking six or seven years. While he was
gone, she said, she would be chaste.[1]

An exception was Chaucer's Wife of Bath, who
was not the kind to postpone anything involving
sex. She had had five husbands and could hardly
wait for the sixth, wondering whether he could
teach her anything new about what, in one of her
more ladylike moments, she called "the olde
daunce." [2]

[1] That she was. And sometimes caught.
[2] Actually she knew all the steps, from first to last, and
was more likely to give lessons than to take them.

In the Middle Ages a feudal lord instead of saying his home was his castle would say his castle was his home. The medieval castle was a good place for sex, because a comely village maiden who caught her liege lord's fancy would have difficulty escaping.[1] The moment he saw her his drawbridge would go up, and she would be unable to leave the castle until it went down again.

[1] Assuming she wished to. She might remain in the castle keep as a kept woman.

Difficulty escaping

Meanwhile his yeomen, doing yeoman service, would watch from the castle turret and tell him whether anyone was coming, such as the girl's father, and if so to hurry it up.

One of the most interesting stories involving a medieval lord concerns Leofric, the Earl of Mercia. When he refused to remit a tax he had imposed on the people of Coventry, his wife Lady Godiva tried all of her wiles on him, and some of them fitted rather well. Finally he said he would remit the tax if she would ride naked through the streets at noonday.[1] She took him at his word, first directing all the good people of Coventry to keep within doors and lower their shutters. Apparently she forgot about the bad people of Coventry, one of whom was a tailor named Peeping Tom, who looked out as Lady Godiva rode by and was struck blind. Interviewed later, P. Tom is quoted as having said, "It was worth it." [2] His tailoring business dropped off sharply, but he had his memories.[3]

[1] A husband who suggests such a thing deserves whatever he gets.

[2] Lady Godiva, being very ladylike, rode sidesaddle, and it was Tom's good luck to be on the right side.

[3] The legend is worldwide. Even China has its Peiping Tom.

Despite the Code of Chivalry, this was an era of dirty stories or *Canterbury Tales*.[1] Almost any story could be told in mixed company—even in front of monks, friars, parsons, and prioresses. In fact these men and women of the cloth listened the most attentively, since this was their only way of learning about sex.[2]

[1] In Italy, Boccaccio wrote *Il Decamerone*. When this was translated into English, some of the spiciest parts were left in the original language to encourage young people to study Italian.

[2] Do you really believe this?

Learning about sex

The sex symbol of the Middle Ages was Queen Guinevere, who was admired by all the knights of King Arthur's court. They all had designs on her.[1]

King Arthur's table was round so that he could keep his eye on Lancelot, Gawain, and the other young fellows. A knight had to get the King's permission to leave the table. "Sire," a knight might ask, "may I absent myself for half an hour?" The King was puzzled that Guinevere would so frequently ask, at the same time, "Sire, may I take off for half an hour?" It never occurred to him to ask, "Take off what?"

Thanks to women like Queen Guinevere and Lady Godiva, chivalry eventually died out, perhaps having been overworked. Sex, however, lived on, and gained robustness in the next era.

[1] Body painting, perhaps with psychedelic patterns, is nothing new.

Round table

Sex symbol

·VI·

SEX IN THE ELIZABETHAN AGE

The sex symbol of the Elizabethan Age was Queen Elizabeth.[1] Her contribution to the history of sex was her ability to remain a virgin or, more accurately, to be called the Virgin Queen. Where Sir Walter Raleigh came in, no one seems to be sure. However the sex play of Sir Walter's placing his cloak in a puddle and letting Elizabeth trample on it was obviously some rare form of fetishism. So also, no doubt, was her having Sir Walter's head cut off, something that gave her great satisfaction.[2]

[1] Queen Elizabeth's age was kept a secret from her courtiers.

[2] See, later, the Marquis de Sade.

The Elizabethan poets sing lustily of sex. Consider Marlowe's "Come live with me and be my love," a brazen proposal of cohabitation. Or, for sheer prurience without redeeming social value, note John Lyly's

> Cupid and my Campaspe played
> At cards for kisses,

which describes the Elizabethan form of strip poker, starting with kisses and leading to no telling what.[1] Spenser, in *The Faerie Queene,* paints an erotic picture of Una, the lovely lady with "an Asse more white than snow," while an anonymous poet [2] urges "Back and side, go bare, go bare," knowing full well that backless and sideless would lead inevitably to frontless, with girls trying to outdo each other.[3]

For a nasty sort of perversion, think for a moment [4] about John Donne's "Get with child a mandrake root." This is almost as unpleasant as Ben Jonson's impudent question, in *The Triumph of Charis:* "Have you tasted the bag of the bee?"

[1] We could tell but have promised not to.
[2] No wonder he would not give his name.
[3] And men trying to undo them.
[4] About as long as anyone can stand.

Elizabethan poet

57

Shakespeare, a product of the Elizabethan Age, was always leering at lovers in compromising situations.[1] In *Hamlet,* for example, he has Polonius say of the Prince, "How pregnant his replies sometimes are." Better Hamlet's replies than Polonius' daughter, at any rate. On another occasion Ophelia comes right out and says to her father, regarding Hamlet, "I denied him access to me." She may have posted a sign saying "Do Not Enter Here" or "Road Closed."

Nor did Shakespeare limit his bawdiness to young lovers. In *The Taming of the Shrew* he describes married sex in such a way as to set matrimony back at least a hundred years. And then, in his *Sonnets,* he tells of his own love for both a dark lady and a dark laddy. Apparently it didn't matter which sex as long as it was dark.[2]

Sex made a noteworthy advance in this period with the invention of a new article of men's clothing, the codpiece. It was often seen on the stage.[3]

---

[1] Some anti-Stratfordians believe that Shakespeare was actually King Lear, and vice versa.

[2] The principle, according to modern sexologists, is that the less you see the more you feel.

[3] And not merely when it fell off.

The codpiece, a bagged appendage later replaced by the zipper, was a kind of male falsie, often promising more than could be delivered. But it helped tell the boys from the girls.[1] In the Elizabethan theater, we are told, "men often took women's parts." Which parts, however, are not specified.

[1] It would be especially useful today.

Married sex

Article of clothing

An interesting reference to use of the codpiece not only as indicative of maleness but as a kind of duffel bag or attaché case is in M. von Bohn's *Modes and Manners in the Sixteenth Century*.[1] As the scholarly author tells us of the codpiece of four hundred years ago: "It served as a pocket in which a gentleman kept his handkerchief and purse, and even oranges, which he would pull out before the ladies' eyes and hand to them."

Here is a scene to fix in one's mind: the gentleman reaching in, groping around, and triumphantly pulling out an orange to present to a tensely expectant young lady. It would probably be a Valencia orange, though he might reach in far enough to extract a navel. "Surprise!" the gentleman would cry as he brought forth the gleaming fruit. And the young lady would be surprised indeed, not knowing what he had in mind, or in hand.[2]

---

[1] Modes were all right, but manners were pretty bad.

[2] One wonders what goodies a gentleman carried around for presentation when oranges were out of season. A bright red apple, perhaps, or a banana. The codpiece, we are told, "diminished in size after 1570," for reasons not explained. In 1604 (a bad year) it disappeared entirely.

Wider horizons

This was the Renaissance when, in the field of sex, new vistas were opened up and people had wider horizons. It was an age of exploration.[1]

One further word. Renaissance is defined as "any period characterized by enthusiastic and vigorous activity along literary, artistic, *or other lines*." (Italics mine.) The writer of this definition, which is full of leering innuendoes, obviously had sex in mind, if not on his mind.[2] Nevertheless the reference to "enthusiastic and vigorous activity" is an accurate description of sex in this lusty era.

[1] Some think the age of exploration is about thirteen.

[2] The definition will be found in that pornographic work, *Webster's New International Dictionary*.

·VII·

SEX IN THE SEVENTEENTH AND EIGHTEENTH CENTURIES

For the next two hundred years, during the Age of Mistresses, sex was dominated by the French.[1] The only blemish in what might have been an unbroken record of illicit sex was Louis XIV's marriage to his mistress, Madame de Maintenon. Cautious about such an unorthodox and un-French act, Louis delayed until he was nearly fifty. Even then, he kept his marriage secret for fear of ridicule by members of his court.[2]

---

[1] Spain, however, had Don Juan. What Don Juan had, we can only guess. It was something that made him irresistible to women.

[2] Members of his court, or courtiers, were always courting, but not with an eye to matrimony. Not with so much else to see.

Louis XIV is called the Sun King, but some historians think this is an error, caused by a reportorial or typographical slip, and it should be Fun King.

Fun king

Louis XV, who came to the throne when he was only five years old, was not at once given a mistress. "Play with these for a while," he was told, and for several years he had to get his kicks by pulling up the dresses of dolls and manikins.[1] But with the completion of his puberty rites,[2] he was considered capable of handling a mistress.

[1] To look at their fanikins.

[2] "I demand my rites!" he shouted, meaning that he felt he was old enough for the real thing.

Louis XV

His first, a living doll, was Madame de Pompadour. With remarkable staying power, she lasted for twenty years, perhaps because she could now and then hide in one of the hundreds of rooms in Versailles and recuperate. Madame de Pompadour was followed by Madame du Barry. It is worth noting that when Louis first met her, she was the mistress of the Comte Jean du Barry. Louis arranged her marriage to the brother of Du Barry, since it was considered more respectable [1] to have a married woman for a mistress.

[1] And more pleasantly sinful.

Replaces Pompadour

Refinements

When it comes to the little refinements and nuances of sex, the French are unrivaled.

With reference to refinements, we should not overlook the Marquis de Sade. This specialist in perversion brought something new to sex, which in his honor was called sadism.[1] Imprisoned for an unnatural act, though he swore he was only doing what came naturally, he wrote some of his best (i.e., most obscene) plays and novels in the Bastille. Thanks to De Sade, the makers of whips, ropes, knives, and brass knuckles saw a profitable rise in their business.[2] A woman with a black eye,

[1] Some people pronounce the word with a long "a" and a long face. Others, using a short "a," make it sound sad. However pronounced, to the Marquis and his followers it was fun. "Don't knock it if you haven't tried it," they said, smiling smugly.

[2] This illustrates what financial experts refer to as the spin-off from sex.

lacerated lips, patches of hair torn out at the roots, scourge marks on her neck and arms, and a bad limp was not looked upon with pity but with envy. Here was a woman who had been loved.[1]

Many will be pleased to know that the Marquis de Sade spent the last twelve years of his life in an insane asylum.[2]

Meanwhile in Italy there was Casanova, who traveled throughout Europe from woman to woman.[3] His contribution to sex was the discovery, made in his *Memoirs,* that (1) it is a good idea to keep moving, and (2) people will believe what you write about your exploits. Those who think that too much sex shortens one's life should remember Casanova. He lived to be seventy-three, which in the eighteenth century was considerably beyond the national average. Moreover during his last years, while he was writing his *Memoirs,* he was savoring his past and, in effect, living twice.

---

[1] Not wisely, perhaps, but too well.

[2] His place in the asylum, if not in history, was secure. He was classified as "an incurable lunatic."

[3] Writing home from Cologne, where he had been having an affair with the burgomaster's wife, he reportedly was the first to say: "Having a wonderful time. Wish you were her."

Some say he enjoyed it even more the second time, with no worry about what was then called the pox or the unexpected return of a jealous husband.

Those were vintage years for sex.[1]

[1] Even if you discount Casanova's narrative by fifty percent, he lived a full life. By the way, in discussing sex in the seventeenth and eighteenth centuries, I have left out the Puritans of New England. Does anyone mind, really?

Savoring his past

On a couch

·VIII·

SEX IN THE
NINETEENTH CENTURY

The nineteenth century was a confusing and con-
tradictory period. The same century that produced Queen Victoria produced Havelock Ellis,
Baron Richard von Krafft-Ebing, Sigmund Freud,
and Jack the Ripper.[1] As far as sex is concerned,
this was a period of flux.

Imagine, if you can, Queen Victoria on a couch
and Dr. Freud seated nearby with a pen and note-
book. Indeed, imagine Queen Victoria on a
couch. Usually she is sitting up very straight, in a
straight chair, her skirt touching the floor and her

---

[1] Not to mention the manufacturers of whalebone stays for
corsets and the hundreds of whales who made their contribution, overlooked by most social historians.

legs crossed or held tightly together.[1] Or consider the scene in her bedroom in Buckingham Palace. "Don't look," she would tell Prince Albert, "I'm getting undressed." Whereupon she would take off her hat and gloves.[2]

Ellis and Krafft-Ebing wrote about sex from the standpoint, respectively, of psychology and neurology. By using technical language and pretending to be scientific, they managed to escape censorship. It was Havelock Ellis who wrote: "Without an element of the obscene there can be no true and deep aesthetic or moral conception of life. . . . It is only the great men who are truly obscene." This was a new way of measuring great-

[1] Some think her fingers were crossed too, but they forget that among Eminent Victorians she was the Pre-eminent Victorian.

[2] Prince Albert would be too busy to look anyhow, admiring his likeness on a can of tobacco.

Bedroom scene

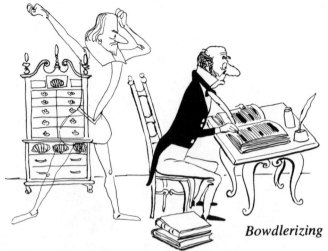

Bowdlerizing

ness. Even Thomas Bowdler would have found it difficult to expurgate the works of Shakespeare had he read such a statement.[1]

Sigmund Freud, the father of modern psychiatry, believed that sex was at the root of everything.[2] It was his contention that sexual impulses date from the cradle, which, as one sexologist says, "is something to think about the next time you see a tiny baby slobbering over a teething ring."

[1] Bowdler died thirty-four years before Havelock Ellis was born. A physician, Bowdler must have known the facts of life, but he saw no reason for others to learn about them.

[2] This may be why some find it dirty.

Had it not been for Freud, we might now tell about our dreams to anyone who would listen, instead of only to a highly paid professional. Were it not for Freud, also, we might think that a small boy's affection for his mother was rather sweet, not knowing that he might have an Oedipus complex and require therapy. Freud made it possible for people to speak knowingly about the ego, super-ego, and id. Previously many had thought *id* an abbreviation of *idem* and somehow related to *ibid*.[1]

[1] Not to mention such sexy expressions as *op. cit., loc. cit.,* and *vide supra.*

Oedipus complex

Thanks to the psychiatry of sex, the average male was now able to worry about whether he was oversexed or undersexed. Even the man in the street knew the difference between a dipsomaniac and a nymphomaniac.[1]

And yet, for all these advances, the century ended on a dubious note with what was called the Mauve Decade. This was when a person was considered naughty who said "naughty." [2] The picture that comes to one's mind when thinking of the *fin de siècle* is of Whistler painting his mother instead of a voluptuous nude, and Oscar Wilde making love to a sunflower.[3]

[1] As for the woman in the street, or street walker, she was probably both.

[2] College students graduating in 1900 made a big thing of being in the class of naughty naught.

[3] He could spend hours pondering its little pistil or stamen, as the case might be.

Fin de siècle

·IX·

SEX TODAY

A relaxed attitude toward sex began shortly after World War I. Even the Kaiser, living in exile in Holland, began to take things easier, removing his helmet while making love.[1]

Ernest Hemingway, Gertrude Stein, Alice B. Toklas, and other members of the Lost Generation found themselves. They found themselves in Paris, living the life of artists in *pensions, ateliers, bistros,* and *pissoirs.* Writers came to grips with life, and some, who had just moved in, came to life with grips. It was one of those fortuitous confluences in history: Paris was full of Americans

[1] It was a fair trade. He would take off his helmet if the girl would take off her wooden shoes.

Came to grips with life

who had the money and Parisians who had the know-how.[1] Something was sure to come of it.[2]

In America, repeal of Prohibition had its effect on sex. A plentiful supply of good liquor made it

[1] Not only the know-how but the cancan.
[2] Something that might require medical attention.

possible for a young man to ply a young woman with drink until she was completely pliable. Loose women, especially, became tight. Some excited young man was forever lifting his glass and saying, "Here's how," even though the woman he was addressing [1] needed no instructions, perhaps having been to Paris herself. However as the Jazz Age drew to a close, it once again became fashionable for a man to drink out of a glass instead of out of a lady's slipper, and this was a blow to shoe fetishists.

[1] Or undressing.

Plied with drink

Talking pictures also had their impact. Movie stars no longer had bee-stung lips,[1] and began to speak for themselves, saying such things as "Yes." Love scenes became more realistic. A woman's pants could now be heard as well as seen.

The stock market crash of 1929 had its effect on sex also. Men jumped out of windows, and not always because they were caught in a compromising situation with their secretary. To offset the effects of the Great Depression, women began to get shots of silicone in their breasts, and men began to feel there was still something to live for.[2]

[1] Thus throwing millions of bees out of work.

[2] Science has not yet been able to do anything comparable for men. The only contribution to masculinity since the codpiece has been padded shoulders.

Became more realistic

Pin-up photo

World War II saw the use of the pin-up photo to make men forget the horrors of combat. Their imaginations were raised to such a pitch that they began to think the girl waiting for them at home looked like Rita Hayworth. They were driven almost insane by the desire to pin down what was pinned up.

Sex made a great leap forward with the famous nude photograph of Marilyn Monroe, who did more not only for sex but for the calendar than anyone since Pope Gregory XIII.[1] Men are known to have looked at a calendar with Marilyn Monroe's photograph on it, to see what day of the month it was, until the day they were looking up was yesterday.

We now have such sex queens as Raquel Welch and Elizabeth Taylor.[2] With them, sex has reached new dimensions.

Young people learn about sex early. Some learn about it from their parents, some from their

[1] Gregory did a lot for the calendar but very little for sex.

[2] Queen Elizabeth II is not a sex queen, or even a very sexy queen.

Early learner

Without going to school

teachers, and some from child-molesters. Having had enough theorizing, many young people go to college to get first-hand (or wherever) experience by living in coeducational dormitories or cohabitational apartments.[1]

Hippies learn about sex without going to school. Mostly they lie around naked, playing with their beads.

[1] Girls living in the latter are known not as coeds but as cohabs.

Mention should also be made of the Pill.[1]

Beginning with the Kinsey Report, this has been the Age of the Poll. Almost any hour of the day or night one may hear a ring of the doorbell and be confronted by a poll-taker [2] with a clip-board, asking such questions as "How many times a day?" "What about holidays?" and "Have you any other hobbies?" When the results of the poll are published, everyone checks his or her percentile and either is elated or makes an appointment for a thorough physical.[3]

Nudity is now very much with us. As someone has said, "Skin is big these days." [4] With nude men and women stimulating [5] the sex act on the stage, it is no longer necessary to strain to look through a keyhole or under a window blind. A Peeping Tom is now a man who sits on the front row with binoculars.

[1] All right, it has been mentioned.

[2] Considering the number that have been taken, it is a wonder there are any left.

[3] What could be the matter? A virus? An allergy? Too much cholesterol?

[4] Beauty is only skin deep, but this is deep enough for any-one not interested in looking at blood vessels, subcutaneous fat, and sebaceous glands.

[5] Pardon the typographical error. It should be "simulating."

Stay-at-home

Or he may stay home, sitting up close to the television set and watching a girl in a commercial soaping herself in a shower or begging, with half-closed eyes and throaty voice, "Take it off. Take it *all* off." The girl is in a delirium of desire from having had a whiff of an aphrodisiac after-shave lotion.

Magazines with photographs of nude women, including an extra-large photo in the centerfold for those with weak eyes, abound. Advertisements suggest [1] further materials, such as home movies, obtainable by mail.[2] When such movies are shown at home, window shades should be pulled down tightly to keep out the light.

[1] Suggestively.

[2] For adults only. After all, only adults need this sort of help.

Topless waitresses provide businessmen with something to look at besides menus and sales charts.

It should be apparent, as we reach the end of this brief history of sex, that forms, manners, and devices have differed through the ages.[1] There were, for instance, no television cameras at the Roman orgies, providing home audiences with instant replay in slow motion. Nor were there mini-togas. But, as was indicated by the disappearance of chastity belts with the advent of the see-through dress, such things are superficial and transitory.[2]

One conclusion is inescapable. The more things change, the more sex remains the same.

As the French would say, *Vive la monotonie!*

[1] Note, however, that Marlowe, writing of Helen of Troy, referred to "the topless towers of Ilium."

[2] Love potions are out and pep pills are in.

Centerfold

ABOUT THE AUTHOR

Richard Armour is one of the most widely read writers of humor and satire in our time. His books, of which this is the forty-second, include a number of best sellers and have been translated into many languages. He has also contributed to more than 200 magazines in the United States and England, from the *Saturday Review* to *Playboy* and from *The New Yorker* to *The Reader's Digest*.

A Harvard Ph.D. and longtime professor of English at many colleges and universities, he has lectured or been guest-in-residence on over 200 campuses. As an American Specialist for the State Department, he has also lectured at leading universities throughout Europe and Asia.

In addition to an amazing variety of subjects, Richard Armour writes in both verse (as in *Light Armour, Nights with Armour,* etc.) and prose, and for children as well as adults. One of his most unusual books is the recent *On Your Marks: A Package of Punctuation,* with a foreword by

Ogden Nash, which has been made into an animated film. He is especially popular with students for such books as *It All Started with Columbus, Twisted Tales from Shakespeare, The Classics Reclassified, American Lit Relit,* and *English Lit Relit,* and with teachers for *Going Around in Academic Circles* and *A Diabolical Dictionary of Education.*

Dr. Armour is married (as you would discover in *My Life with Women* and *Through Darkest Adolescence*) and lives in Claremont, California.

ABOUT THE
ILLUSTRATOR

Campbell Grant, who has illustrated eleven of Richard Armour's books, was with Walt Disney for twelve years as a character creator and story man. During World War II he worked with Frank Capra on documentaries. He is the illustrator of many books for children and adults and has done the drawings for the book version of many Disney films. Since 1960 he has been actively interested in archaeology, and has recorded and made paintings of the aboriginal rock paintings in the Santa Barbara mountains and published many articles on the subject. In 1965 his first book was published, *The Rock Paintings of the Chumash*. It was picked as one of the top 25 books of the year for outstanding design at the 1966 American Association of University Presses book show. Later he broadened the scope of the study to include the rock art of North America, and his recently published *Rock Art of the American Indian* is the definitive book on the subject. He teaches art at a nearby private school, travels widely, and is active in conservation matters. Living idyllically on a ranch near Santa Barbara, he raises avocados and has a talented writer-wife and four children.